# Playing Fields

# Playing Fields

Poems by

Joseph Chelius

© 2025 Joseph Chelius. All rights reserved.
This material may not be reproduced in any form, published,
reprinted, recorded, performed, broadcast,
rewritten, or redistributed without
the explicit permission of Joseph Chelius.
All such actions are strictly prohibited by law.

Cover design by Shay Culligan
Cover photo by Joseph Chelius and Patricia Griffin-Chelius
Author photo by Patricia Griffin-Chelius
Proofreading, department of editorial glitches, by Sharyl Wolf

ISBN: 978-1-63980-753-6

Kelsay Books
502 South 1040 East, A-119
American Fork, Utah 84003
Kelsaybooks.com

*for Patricia, Sarah, and Andrew*

# Acknowledgments

Thank you to the following publications, in which versions of these poems previously appeared:

*3rd Wednesday:* "Centipede in the Kitchen Sink," "Cold Symptoms While Walking at Lunch"
*Arts & Cultural Council of Bucks County. 30 Days of Inspiration:* "On Political Divide"
*Autumn Sky Poetry DAILY:* "Fly"
*Bucks County Herald* (The Poet's Corner): "Old Green Sofa"
*Cider Press Review:* "Playing Catch"
*Dulcet:* "Root Vegetable Soup"
*Little Free Lit Mag:* "Little Free Libraries"
*Moonstone Press:* "Pandemic Days: Working from Home"
*Neshaminy:* "Bird Blind"
*ONE ART:* "Stopping Between Errands to Watch Little League Baseball," "The Franklin Institute"
*Paterson Literary Review:* "Fifteen," "Itinerant's Song," "The Corner Study"
*Philadelphia Stories:* "Street Impressions"
*Schuylkill Valley Journal:* "Delinquency," "Manual Push Mower Saved from Scrap," "Purchasing Brahms, Symphony #3, at the Campus Store," "Scrubbing the Chili Pot," "Smokey Gray," "The Baffle," "The Other Guy," "Walking Lake Caroline"
*Spitball:* "Inventing the Mind's Playground," "Johnny Callison," "Pimple Ball," "Pop-Up"
*The Sunlight Press:* "At a Turnpike Rest Stop with My Grown Son"
*THINK:* "Dismantled Swing Set," "Little Card"
*The Twin Bill:* "Wearing My Father's Mitt"

With gratitude to my family and friends, my teachers, my former work colleagues, editors of journals, and the Bucks County Poetry Community that has helped sustain my work throughout the years.

# Contents

Delinquency                                         13

I. Pole, Hydrant, Crushed Tin Can

Street Impressions                                  17
Alex the Shoe Shiner                                18
Grocery Run                                         19
Corner Drugstores                                   20
The Franklin Institute                              21
Summer High Jinks                                   22
Pimple Ball                                         23
Pop-Up                                              24
Wearing My Father's Mitt                            25
Johnny Callison                                     26
Friends                                             27
Jumped                                              28
Tom at the Playground                               29
Safety Post                                         31
Bubbles                                             33
Here and There                                      34

II. Chalked Baselines, Clipped Infield Grass

The Yellow Bucket                                   39
Genius Thoughts                                     40
The Little Drummer Boy                              41
The Saturday Hamburgers                             42
Roughage                                            44
Unstoppable                                         45
Mayberry Nights                                     46
Cornmeal Mush                                       47

| | |
|---|---|
| Fifteen | 48 |
| Teasing Mother | 49 |
| Tackle Football | 50 |
| Fly | 51 |
| The Other Guy | 52 |
| Herb Alpert & The Tijuana Brass | 54 |
| Purchasing Brahms, Symphony No. 3, at the Campus Store | 55 |

III. House and Yard

| | |
|---|---|
| The Corner Study | 59 |
| Old Green Sofa | 60 |
| Dismantled Swing Set | 61 |
| Blue Bowling Ball Behind the Shed | 62 |
| Dragonfly on the Screen Door | 63 |
| Manual Push Mower Saved from Scrap | 64 |
| Plastic Bag Entwined in the Maple | 65 |
| Song Sparrow | 66 |
| Pandemic Days: Working from Home | 67 |
| The Baffle | 69 |
| Centipede in the Kitchen Sink | 70 |
| Smokey Gray | 71 |
| Scrubbing the Chili Pot | 73 |
| Inventing the Mind's Playground | 74 |
| Little Card | 75 |
| Root Vegetable Soup | 76 |

IV. Neighborhood, Town, and County

| | |
|---|---|
| Walking Lake Caroline | 81 |
| With Plaid Thermos While Waiting for a Train | 83 |

| | |
|---|---|
| Cold Symptoms While Walking at Lunch | 84 |
| Power Wash | 85 |
| Stopping Between Errands to Watch Little League Baseball | 86 |
| Dog Decoys | 88 |
| Playing Catch | 89 |
| At a Turnpike Rest Stop with My Grown Son | 91 |
| At the Super 8 | 92 |
| Itinerant's Song | 94 |
| Errands with My Father | 95 |
| Mottled Scarf Clinging to Bushes | 97 |
| White Delivery Truck Caught in Branches | 98 |
| Little Free Libraries | 99 |
| The Indian Neighbors | 100 |
| Bird Blind | 101 |
| On Political Divide | 102 |

# Delinquency

The wind on my block is so unruly
this afternoon—
kicking over trash barrels
and hollering obscenities
into a row of empty mailboxes—
that I can't help remembering a time
when it was content simply
to traipse through the flowers
and was always mindful
of people's property.
Alas, it was a little breeze then.

# I.
# Pole, Hydrant, Crushed Tin Can

# Street Impressions

*Chester Avenue, Southwest Philadelphia, early 1960s*

As on a children's show,
the green-and-cream trolley
with wide windows for eyes,
an emblem above the headlight
like a little mustache,
would come into view—
its doors hissing open, then closed
before it went hiccupping
over the cobblestone tracks.

And down the back alley
past Rusty the Boxer
and Bunky the Beagle,
stirred up along the hairpin fences,
the songs of hucksters
carrying splintered baskets
of freestone peaches
and Jersey tomatoes;
the neighborly chatter
of clothes on the lines.

And the characters we'd meet
along the avenue:
Alex the shoe shiner
and John the milkman;
palsied Mr. Packer
with his handcart of Schmidt's.
The older boys, who with sycamore pods
they gathered from the curbs
to chalk their lessons—
scrawled in cursive
on the slates of our necks.

# Alex the Shoe Shiner

Each day we'd find him
in his little booth,
a stooped man of color
(colored, then)
who in a plaid jeff cap,
a smock smudged
black and brown,
shined the shoes
of customers behind the wall
of *The Evening Bulletin*
and *The Daily News*.
"Hi, Alex," we'd say
as we'd run through the booth—
not to taunt
but just to hear his "Hiya" back,
neither looking up, nor missing
a beat with the brush
as he'd send us
into the sunshine again,
pleased to think
that our permission
to call him by his first name—
if permission it was—
meant we were friends,
that we knew him well.

# Grocery Run

*Paul Brothers, Unity-Frankford Store, 58th and Chester*

The other brothers seemed fixed
in their places: at the cold meat slicer,
the ancient cash register,
but fidgety Nate, in a wrinkled smock
and black-framed glasses,
played the free agent—
roved the whole floor
in a waft of Old Gold.
Over the scuffed linoleum tiles
I'd follow close
as he'd pluck from the shelves
with metal grabbers
each random item I'd be sent to buy:
sauerkraut, Campbell's Pork & Beans.
Then, with a deft little flip
("Here, kid. Careful not to mash.")
a loaf of Sunbeam bread I'd cradle
like a football, still trying to keep up
as I'd cut right, then left, eluding
the pickle barrel, a woman in a sequined hat,
the Bon Ton chips man
maneuvering through the doorway
a tower of snacks on a red handcart,
the door thumping closed with the music of bells.

# Corner Drugstores

Waiting in line at a CVS,
some generic pop tune
piped through a speaker,
I think of the staid order
of corner drugstores,
as ubiquitous as taverns
on the rowhouse blocks.
At Boonan's, the checkerboard tiles
and behind polished glass
apothecary jars in walnut cases;
the remedies of comic books, Fudgsicles,
Life Savers, Charms.

And through seasons of flu,
their measured touches
as familiar as trademarks:
Mr. Fleisher, the knot of his tie
visible under the white lab coat,
a Philly blunt jutting from his mouth
as he filled the prescriptions
my mother had sent for,
bringing to the register
his clinking potions—
cough syrup with codeine,
fever medicine that burned like whiskey—
in crimped brown bags.

In a jar on the counter,
Rold Gold pretzels
as straight as sentries—
his sending me off
with a wink and a rod.

# The Franklin Institute

*for Mary Rita Higgins Chelius*

All the wonders of science and invention
stood before us in the distance: if only
we could decode the pattern of the Parkway lights—
our grandmother in her green coat and hat,
the scent of Jean Naté,
leading the three of us with our blond crew cuts
on the day's expedition: the trolley ride
into town; soft pretzels from a vendor.
And then, as amused Ben Franklin looked on,
peering through his tiny spectacles,
our stepping into the crosswalk—
the talk so many years later
not of the Planetarium, or even the Giant Heart,
but our awe of tall buildings, the bewildering
phenomenon of commerce and traffic;
our linking hands as if entering
a panorama—sun glinting off metal and chrome.

# Summer High Jinks

So we wouldn't rot all summer
in front of the TV,
our mothers sent the two of us out
those humid Philadelphia mornings to pester
the milkman with his metal crates,
bottles clinking up the rowhouse steps.
To stamp on the flat cellar doors
outside groceries and taverns,
collect from pay phones along the avenue
loose change we'd spend on candy and gum.
At Myers Rec, we'd taunt the 58$^{th}$ Street gang
who, if in the mood, would chase us
across the fields and courts,
past the spinner and slide,
and once, with nowhere to run,
to the top of the fire escape stairs of the Rec building
where they dangled us by our ankles—
in our terror the hoops and rides
tilted upside down, the concrete below
a sparkling pool.

# Pimple Ball

*Kingsessing, Southwest Philadelphia, 1960s*

Plain as a potato, with tiny pustules
along the rubbery skin, it sustained us
through our summer games
of step-ball, wire-ball, sock-it-out.

At a chalked strike zone, it could lend pizzazz
to a kid in sneaks who bested his records
in the empty stadium of MBS schoolyard—
transformed at the wall into Bunning and Short.

Or make discourse along Chester Avenue—
a bouncy exchange
with Alex the shoe shiner,
buffing leather in his shingled hut;

the cook at Vittle Vat in his red bandana
as he stood at the grill
before a hill of onions, a mound of chipped steak—
his percussive spatula shiny with grease.

When it got gashed or torn, how resourceful
we became—like moms in rowhouse kitchens,
serving up halfies, with broomsticks our utensils,
a crushed soda can for a plate.

# Pop-Up

Requisite drama of two outs, the bases loaded,
and up to the plate steps the Warriors' weakest hitter,
the cross of the bat heavy on his shoulder, wobbly
helmet blocking his view.
Perhaps it is the innocence in his face—
the heart-rending vulnerability—
that convinces Coach Halpin,
crouching with his clipboard,
an unfiltered Chesterfield between his fingers,
not to summon him back, but to rouse the whole team
into cheering him on. Knees trembling,
he watches pitches stream past,
then swings and connects—
sends a soft fly the Spartans' first baseman,
like a drowsy spider, snags in his web.
On rounding the bag, he receives from Coach Gannon,
stationed at first, an attaboy and a fanny whack.
And on his return to the bench, he finds the spirit still going—
boys who all season long had spurned his play
caught up in the drama, a camaraderie they hadn't known,
propelled by kindness as they pounded his back.

# Wearing My Father's Mitt

*A Trapper Model*

Without his knowing I wore it that spring
while playing the outfield—
my father's lefthander's first baseman's mitt
I'd found buried among rollers and paint cans
under the workbench in the cellar,
mending the laces with knotted twine.
On the wrong hand it felt clumsy,
but when the ball would come my way
I'd drift under it and catch
aslant—a minor skill I'd developed
as if imagining he'd stop by the field
in the middle of a workday to watch for a while,
his hands shifting on the handle of his briefcase
before he nodded approval and turned away.
That his seeing me with his glove—
which had grown soft and pliant—
might loosen his stance, even ease
the tension that filled the kitchen
when he returned from the high school
with its faculty and students,
that undermining superintendent, steam
from our plates rising as we ate.
That I'd recover from out in left field
my father as a boy
on the sandlot greens of Yeadon, Pennsylvania,
his body lithe and unfettered—
scooping throws around the first base bag.

# Johnny Callison

*Little Americans' bus trip to Connie Mack Stadium, late 1960s*

In the right field bleachers at Connie Mack,
the Little Americans are calling out
to their favorite player as he trots on the field, puzzled
when he won't look up—won't smile or wave.
At eight and nine they are too young to imagine
that a star from a town as modest
as Qualls, Oklahoma, might shy from attention
as from a high and tight pitch.
Or brood over his last at-bat,
wondering all the while about his diminishing power—
home run totals like plummeting degrees.
Better as they sit like recruits in their LA caps
to occupy themselves with the sights around them—
the pristine field, the Ballantine sign,
the vendors with their silver carts.
Better to wait for the teams to change sides
so they can shout *Hey, Henry!*
to the Braves' Hank Aaron, who slips them
an obliging wave before the inning gets underway
and he settles into position—
hands on knees, as their coaches taught.

# Friends

When the first colored family
moved onto our block,
we accepted Ronnie into our games.
In striped tee shirts that exposed
an inner tube of brown belly,
he was soft all over—
from the outfield lofted his throws
and poked humpbacked drives,
chugged the bases on his flabby legs.
And when the games were over
his gentleman's habit:
"Friends," he'd say, and shake our hands.

So that day we argued
and he bopped me in the nose,
I felt more betrayed than injured—
as if Stymie or Buckwheat
in the *Our Gang* reruns
had shown a meaner side.
"Friends," he said, as the blood
trickled out and I fought back
tears while turning away.
"Friends," he persisted
until I finally relented—
his moist palm
plump and strange.

# Jumped

*April 1968*

No matter our ages,
only nine or ten
and the blade he drew—
no bigger than my pinky—
glanced off the ribs
of my puffy green jacket.
Or that a kid nearby
ran for his father,
a kindly man
who spoke to us equally—
made us look each other in the eye,
and even shake hands.
It was enough for me
in school the next day
to boast to the tough kids
I'd been jumped in the playground,
one of the coloreds
avenging the death of that
Martin Luther King guy,
taking it out on the white kids.
Because of him.

# Tom at the Playground

He'd turn up around four
in sandals and shorts
and set his lawn chair
on top of the climber—
taking the sun,
as he liked to say,
using words like *divine* and *lovely*
to describe the weather,
then open his *Daily News*.
None of us minded,
even found it peculiar—
this fellow from the neighborhood
who kept his hair neat
and shirts tucked in,
who spoke to us
in the voice of our teachers,
asking about our families,
our favorite foods.
No one could picture him
tossing a football
or swinging a bat.
Or could say which house
he lived in,
what he did for work—
whether, like our fathers,
our older brothers,
he worked at all.
We'd go back to our play,
getting into fights,

pushing each other too hard
on the spinner and swings,
forgetting he was there,
the words we would learn—
not lovely, not divine—
still a few years away.

# Safety Post

Wearing our floppy patrol belts,
we were sent out early
by the Immaculate Heart nuns
to stand on corners with our arms

as fixed as wooden gates
we raised, then lowered
as we shepherded little ones
across the street.

But that day of the fight
along Chester Avenue we ducked
inside the candy store
as bricks and bottles

crossed the tracks,
soon a patrol of police
with clubs and badges
sending the white kids

one way, hollering threats,
and the blacks the other,
hollering back. Young ourselves
we watched at the window

with candy we'd bought—
jawbreakers, red licorice
as if to wait out a storm
or pick up a signal

it was safe enough
to enter a crosswalk—
to leave our refuge
and report to our posts.

# Bubbles

*for David M., victim of the race wars of Kingsessing,
in Southwest Philadelphia; March 1972*


As I went house to house
with my morning *Inquirers,*
all I wanted after taking it in
was to give him back
his mid-range jumper and modest
sky hook, his plodding steps
when he drove to the rim.
To restore him in the MBS school colors—
white shirt, maroon tie—
to his place in the middle:
in alphabetical rows, the average track,
the May processions—
when from shortest to tallest
the Immaculate Heart sisters lined us up.
To delete the headline,
or at least soften the verbs
(*killed* over a dime,
*stabbed* two blocks from home)
and with it the unlikeliness
of his front-page photo:
the dimpled cheeks, the curly hair
that gave him his nickname,
Bubbles, *a friend to all,*
a boy no less ordinary than I was,
who that morning on a suburban corner,
two years after moving away,
settled onto my shoulder the weighty bag of folded papers,
then set off on my route to carry the news.

# Here and There

> *What are you doing here?*
> —Friend's greeting when I visited the old neighborhood

By here, I suppose,
he could only have meant
the makeshift bases
of pole and hydrant,
of crushed tin can;
old sneaks on a wire,
treading the breeze.
The hoagie shops
and corner taverns—
fried onions, stale lager
on passing by.
Or the rival gangs
with bricks and bottles;
the three-day race wars,
the sheltering in.

And there, the chalked
baselines, clipped
infield grass;
the asphalt courts
with nets on the rims.
My two friends and me
with our ten-speed bikes;
our awkward talk;
the looks we exchanged—
tacit, uneasy—
when at the top of the block
the black teens appeared.
Then our taking leave—

barely saying goodbye—
when in single file
we pedaled away
from here back to there
with me in between.

II.
Chalked Baselines, Clipped Infield Grass

# The Yellow Bucket

On our trips in the station wagon—
those rides along winding suburban roads
in our flight from the city, the search for a bigger house—
it traveled with us like a family pet,
wedged on the floor of the passenger seat,
its handle vibrating between my mother's feet.
When one of us groaned—
my father worked up in traffic
or lost again, spinning us in circles—
she'd turn from the crumpled map in her lap
to swipe it under a chin.
Later, scrubbed out with Spic and Span,
it gleamed in its custodian's uniform,
ready for the next trip—
maybe to a movie, the seashore,
my father in his summer clothes,
the clunky black dress shoes replaced
by the canvas sneaks he rarely wore,
dragged out from under the bed;
sneaks that were spry on the pedals,
executing between gas and brake
their nifty two-steps, a delicate dance.

# Genius Thoughts

For a time in the fifth grade
my hair was so short
the kids called me *Eggy*—
stopping at my desk
on their way down the aisle
to rub the orb of my head
as if for good luck.
Big joke to my parents
when I complained at home.
And my grandmother, turning pages
of her *Catholic Standard,* said,
"Why don't you tell them
that eggheads are geniuses?"
Sure, as if I didn't have trouble enough—
tracking fly balls, being attentive in class.
Best to let it blow over, I thought,
as I started my homework.
They'll get bored, eventually—
move to somebody else.
Science was hard that night,
and math concepts befuddling.
Under a dim fluorescence
I brooded at the kitchen table—
with tender fingers massaged my scalp.

# The Little Drummer Boy

On the family console
it crackled and skipped,
none of us fazed
by the gaudy orchestration—
its choir and strings—
as we helped decorate
the house for Christmas,
setting up the electric candles,
the homely Nativity
my mother had constructed
from old playpen parts.

But that day Miss Caputo
cued it up on the school's
musty box phonograph
and the boys around me
began to snicker, my ears tingled
as I heard it anew:
those lofty voices—
its corny rum-pum-pum-pums—
revealing my family to be
if not strange or offbeat,
then hopelessly out of step.

# The Saturday Hamburgers

*for Alice Daly Meehan*

Around the table no one complained
that the hamburger patties
my grandmother formed

as gingerly as a kid
shaping a snowball—
the raw ground beef

frigid to the touch—
were lumpish, spheroidal,
too squat for the buns.

We ate them with relish
and an economy-sized bag
of Wise potato chips, my parents

preoccupied with a day's tasks;
and the six of us siblings
still learning to grasp

in her swollen knuckles,
the bent arthritic fingers,
the language of hands

in a shadowy kitchen;
one as if in commiseration,
a sisterly fortitude,

folded over the other
as they labored at the cutting board,
chopping carrots and cucumber,

pausing in the late afternoon
to knead the stiffness from her throbbing joints
before pressing on again.

# Roughage

After my grandfather died,
this new word *roughage*
came into our house,
my father bringing endive, arugula,
the wood chip tang
of Kretschmer's wheat germ
he'd sprinkle on bran flakes
like a magical dust
to dispel what lurked
in the colon's interiors:
the conspiracies among cells,
their hidden agendas,
my grandfather gone
a year into his retirement
from Bell Telephone,
and my father silent, disconnected,
taking in roughage
those mornings before work.

# Unstoppable

On my best day playing
I cracked two doubles,
then bit off a smile
when on my third time up
the other team's coach
waved his outfielders back.
*There,* I thought,
when I connected again—
driving a ball to deep center,
almost clearing the fence.
And *there* and *there,*
when at the hot corner
I nabbed a line drive
and tagged out the runner
who had strayed off base.
I was unstoppable that day,
having dedicated this game
to my grandfather in Yeadon
as he sat emaciated in a chair.

*Do a good job for me,*
he had murmured
when my brother and I
came to cut his grass.
*Do a good job,* but the cancer
in his colon had advanced
in the standings.
It had gained momentum—
was unstoppable too.

# Mayberry Nights

It never took much, the laughter
percolating in his chest
then bubbling over
those nights after supper
we watched reruns of *Andy Griffith*
with its town full of Goobers
and stammering Floyds.

How it pleased us to see:
our giddy dad, the dropped decorum,
so different from the brooding sheriff
we encountered each morning
in a chair in the corner,
who with a mug of coffee
he took without sugar
guarded his solitude
that hour before work.

# Cornmeal Mush

Not squishy or soft
as I might have supposed
from the *Our Gang* reruns
we watched on UHF,
but with the heft of a brick
I could carve into slices
and fry on the stove
till they crisped at the edges—
sit half-submerged
in a lake of Log Cabin.
So, on a whim, for novelty
I brought some home,
I was surprised all over
by my father's response—
the anger in him rising
*(What are you, being smart?)*
as if like Spanky and Alfalfa
in Depression years,
he'd be made to eat
his mush again.
And, while he was at it,
cut strips for hose ball
as his kids in the '70s,
buzzed on Froot Loops,
on Lucky Charms,
pedaled on summer days
to the mown fields
of Melson's Track
with their bats and balls
and deep-pocketed gloves
fixed to the handlebars
of their Stingray bikes.

# Fifteen

*for John*

Friday night, in their secret place
above the garage,
my brother and his friends
in jeans and denim jackets
were like workers after hours—
lighting Marlboros, sipping Schlitz—
when the door rolled open
and my father, below,
began talking to himself.
How he missed the drift
of smoke and sound overhead,
I'll never know, only that my brother,
when those first words landed—
spattered like drops from a turning sky—
became a teen again
as he ordered his friends
to escape through the window, certain
it was better to risk being caught
with beer and smokes
than have his friends listen in
to his father's patter,
and him without cover—
embarrassed, and exposed.

# Teasing Mother

My son had it down: begin with a stroll
or resounding two-step
from the top of the stairs
before the cry and sudden tumble,
his mother who'd been dicing an onion
or watering a plant
on the scene in seconds to find him
sitting unmaimed on a bottom stair—
flashing a prankster's grin.

And my brothers and me who'd drape
flannels and socks over the crackling
electric log in the fireplace grate, poking fun
at our mother's dread of kerosene—
a lit match, the house in flames—
all the while taking for granted
the clean clothes and regular meals,
a blizzard of college financial aid forms
across her desk as we simulated
the warming of hands at a blaze in the woods—
pretended to be rugged men.

# Tackle Football

Easy to confess what I couldn't
have then: the dread
I'd felt. Each team with maybe
six to a side, facing off.
No helmets or pads,
just a ragged patch
between the baseball fields
with rocks and matted grass.
When the ball was kicked,
I'd look intent as I raced
down field, circumventing
the receiver if he cut my way,
afraid not so much
of hitting, or of being hit,
but of taking hold
of another boy's body:
the intimacy
of wrapping him in my arms,
the two of us tangled,
in a lurid heap, so close
I could whiff on his shirt,
on his dungarees the laundry soap
his mother used—
a fresh and flowery scent.

# Fly

Paid a nickel for every fly
that was foolish enough
to come into our house,
I'd prowl the rooms
with the bent swatter
we hung on a pegboard
by the cellar stairs,
wait till they'd land
on a counter or screen
before I'd sneak up behind
to snuff them out.
No remorse about killing;
nickels were scarce
and we were a fly-free zone.
But once, after zapping one
from a lampshade, I knelt
to see it twitching on the carpet—
a stunned pilot peering out at me
through the windows of its goggles,
looking so weak and vulnerable
I scooped it onto the gurney
of a flattened cereal box
and ferried it through the house,
watching as it roused itself,
dazed but recovering
before I gave a little shake
to send it into the sunshine
through the slightest chink
I made with the door.

# The Other Guy

*for Tom Daly, master plumber*

My uncle, the plumber, found fault
with the shoddy workmanship
of the other guy—
the one who'd come before
to replace the valve, or fix
the leak in the dripping faucet.
On his knees, he'd get up slowly—
a big man with a brogue
and a supply of green tee shirts
whose pockets sagged
like chagrined mouths—
to lecture on the mechanism
of the toilet, pointing out the little things—
the extra pains—
the other guy in his laziness or haste
had ignored or overlooked.
As I'd listen, it was easy to imagine
where the other guy lived:
Rusted trailer, old cars in the yard
as he scratched his belly
and swayed in a hammock,
a six-pack of tall boys
in the unmown grass.
And all the while my uncle,
that crusader, would be off
on his next job, his new van
already weighed down
with pipes and parts—

the equipment he carried
to fix what needed fixing,
and across the county
to undo what had been done.

## Herb Alpert & The Tijuana Brass

My father brought them home,
an aunt in rhinestone frames
cleaning out her cornball collection
I'd stack onto a portable player
as square and musty
as a box suitcase.
Who needed The Beatles
when I could carry these tunes—
everything "Lollipops and Roses"
in the middle of math
or as I floundered at bat.

In time, I put them aside
for the Boss Jock jabber of WFIL,
losing track even of the famous cover
of the woman in whipped cream,
her fey glance and long-stemmed flower
fading under mounds of clothes
on my bedroom floor.

At Krill's on 69th Street
after buying new records
we'd wear out at home—
Creedence Clearwater Revival,
The Beatles, gone solo,
like brothers who have moved away
to lives of their own—
we'd stop in the stores
to play the old gags:
spray perfume at Kresge's,
spin the lunch counter stools.

# Purchasing Brahms, Symphony No. 3, at the Campus Store

I liked the sound of his name,
the chiming chord of its one syllable.
And his caricature on the cover:
in flood pants and a frumpy coat,
the Old Testament beard, stub
of cigar jutting out of his mouth.

And when I purchased it for just $2.99
and played it on the turntable at home,
I was struck by the allegro's *Now hear this,*
as described on the liner notes—
the lush sweep
of Fritz Reiner and the Chicago Symphony Orchestra
becoming my gateway
to classical music's more intricate stuff—
piano trios and string quartets.

And the gateway to my father,
who dismissed everything from Aerosmith to Zeppelin
as *noise* or *crap.* Sitting low
by the big console in the living room,
he would listen to Bach and Handel
while he graded exams or savored a Pabst.
But now my sudden interest
had roused him from his corner,
eager to talk classical music with a son
who for whole afternoons once orchestrated
in the concert hall of his bedroom
games with baseball cards,
a pair of red dice.

And who even as a student in college—
reading literature, buying his first classical records—
still went around composing
lineups in his head—
imagining Brahms in a batting order
with the other stars of his day:
Dickens, Dvořák, Tolstoy, Tchaikovsky.

And on this side of the Atlantic,
culled from the North American League,
that power-hitting tandem
of Melville and Whitman,
who in any lineup of world literature and music
could bat third and cleanup—
even on the 19$^{th}$ century's all-bearded team.

# III.
# House and Yard

# The Corner Study

Sundays after supper my father
went to his makeshift study—
that cramped corner of the living room
where in a rust-colored chair
he graded papers in his lap,
placing by the vase on the console
or the desktop of the radiator
his finished work in disheveled stacks.

Yet years later with the house opened up—
the six of us grown and moved away—
he kept the same study,
requiring nothing more, it seemed,
than this retreat in the corner
where with a mug of coffee
he read *The Inquirer* or sorted mail:
scholar of the bank statement
and insurance claim.

In early light he took in the breeze
as he sat by the windows,
staking this hour alone
with the doves and cardinals,
the finches at the feeder
before a car, a mower,
the arrival of company
could intrude on his study—
before a day made claims
with balances due.

# Old Green Sofa

Before the haulers arrived,
we sat for the last time
on its shabby cushions—
tentative now, on opposite ends,
like strangers at a depot,
awaiting a bus. Agleam,
it had stood out once,
set down among thrift store
purchases, along the beige walls,
on the ancient wool carpet—
immense on its floral seas.
And in so many photos a backdrop,
a hub: Christmases, birthdays,
strewn with wrapping;
in the frivolity of company
with beer and chips;
through late movies, long innings,
a place of respite, a place of comfort—
a bed for our dying cat.
When turned on its side
by a pair of young guys
in backwards caps, it left us
crumbs, a rainfall of change,
the stub of a pencil, an empty space.

# Dismantled Swing Set

Even with the windows closed
we could hear through the house
the shrieks of the Sawzall,
feel the teeth of its blade
as the young neighbor we paid
to remove from the yard
our rusty old swing set
severed without an anesthetic
the limbs of its poles
from those boxy clogs
of hardened cement.

And after stacking everything
into a neat heap at the curb
leaving me to fill the holes
with wood chips I gathered
from a stump in the field,
tamping with a trowel
so when I settled in the evening
with tea or a beer
I would have a clear view
of my son in overalls,
sending his trucks down the ramp
of the slide; and of my swinging
daughter, the lilt of her songs
still faint in the air.

# Blue Bowling Ball Behind the Shed

For the good of order, I am out here again
with a refuse bag and loose-handled scythe—
stumbling over this blue-speckled ball
that hides like a prankster in a thicket of weeds.
How it has come to be outside, and for how many seasons,
I cannot say exactly, but on a whim this year—
when I give in to the urge to pick it up—
I find it lighter than I had imagined,
even hollowed out, the fingerholes with scummy water
that discourages the notion I try testing my form—
arm swung back to roll a strike.

Bring it to the curb for Monday's collection?
The sentimental side of me
(grown more expansive every year)
already feels sorry—
envisions it as a piece of hard candy,
a blue jawbreaker the truck will grind up.

So no, not today at least. Let it endure
another season. Think of it in a different time,
before these slipped-down days,
when it lived in splendor
with the orange hazard cone and No Loitering sign,
the three on a green remnant in my son's bedroom,
joining up with guitar and amp,
the mic on the stand,
to form The Itinerants—a rising punk band
whose themes of non-conformity, of anti-establishmentarianism,
shook up if not the whole country,
then this corner of the world.

# Dragonfly on the Screen Door

After the storm battered the house,
I found it high on the screen
with its wings outstretched,
its head in the beady helmet
perhaps filled with wonder, a tiny relief
at having piloted its vintage plane
(like those seen in museums and on PBS)
through its harrowing flight.

But here in a sudden sun,
it resembled even more
a brooch or a pin
on the mesh of a shirt—
tinted gold, then green,
then gold again—
garish, almost, in the morning light.

# Manual Push Mower Saved from Scrap

When the wheels grew wobbly
and the blades lost their bite,
I retired it under the dogwood tree.
Small recompense, I thought,
for years of service—
its fealty to the grass—
to repurpose it as a lawn ornament
I could see from the window,
looking picturesque when it glistened
in rain or wore a beard of snow.

But within weeks a plain gray spider
spun a web in the blades.
There, crouched in a corner,
it kept perfectly still,
appearing almost ornamental itself
as it awaited a tremor
to dispatch the freight of its body
on thin, high-stepping limbs that advanced
without rancor or pity—
no time for decor.

# Plastic Bag Entwined in the Maple

Another generation of leaves
has grown and passed on,
yet high in the branches
it still clings to its limb
like flesh to bone, persisting
through the kinds of days
that unsettle the wind chimes
and make the chairs go penitent
around the outdoor table—
bow to the edges as if in prayer.
Each year it turns grayer,
shriveled wisp that vanishes
in a hammock of green
only to emerge in fall
when the tree is bare,
wrapped even tighter
as if to have us believe
as it flaps and shudders
in the flippancy of things
that defy the seasons—
hackles raised in the icy air.

# Song Sparrow

*March 2020; pandemic, first days*

After it sailed into the vista
of our storm door, and lay fluttering
among shriveled coleuses
in a bed of brown leaves,
we spoke of omens,
worried over breakfast
about the unlikely prospects
for a bird in the open:
a gift for the ferals
on their morning rounds.

But when we went back later
to find it had vanished,
and on listening close
noted singing in the pines,
it was easy to imagine it
regaling for the others—
still dazed and disbelieving—
the two of us settling
to our reading
if not wholly assured
then as novices in a course
who grasp at symbols—
navigating chapters
in some unwieldy text.

# Pandemic Days: Working from Home

At their morning aquatics,
a pair of squirrels take dives
into puddles from the hostas
we planted by the pines
along the fence—
each supple leaf
a board springing back.

And under the maple
the neighbors' cat
who like a café patron
turns up at the same hour—
always without a book or a tablet—
sits politely at the table
as if awaiting service.
Perhaps we can offer
the day-old salmon
at a marked-down price.

With time and practice,
a mug of warmed-over coffee,
I could learn to like this:
become a student at the window,
or in this case the sliding glass door—
in tune with the playlists
of birds, the way moss
in sizzling August
browns at the edges
like an egg on a stove.

Locate the precise moment
the wandering sun—
as if weary of its own rays—
yawns and stretches,
finds a place in the shade.

# The Baffle

From the kitchen window
I watched the drama
unfold in the yard:
the first squirrel sizing it up
on the pole of the feeder
before he scurried off—I supposed
to get a ladder or tell his friends.
Then another approached,
and another, and though
it was easy for me to gloat—
satisfied, for the sake of the birds,
to have outwitted them at last,
it saddened me, too,
to see them turned away
like patrons at a diner.
And to no longer witness
their stunning acrobatics—
scampering up the pole
before leaping onto the feeder,
rocking it this way and that
as they hung upside down,
their shameless gluttony
on full display.
So I went out again
with my bag of seed,
interfering, as I always did,
and wondering why it was
I could never feel just
one way about a thing,
my arm making little half circles
as I showered the ground.

# Centipede in the Kitchen Sink

*for my daughter Sarah, who shares my birthday*

Because it was our birthday
and I felt kindly toward the world,
I shut off the faucet to save it
from capsizing in its little boat,
the thin oars of its limbs
in rowing away
almost caught in a swirl
down the rapids of the drain
until in my great magnanimity—
a god in a flannel robe—
I gathered it in a paper towel
so I could set it adrift
on the pond of the lawn.
It paused as if to set its course—
uncertain but surely filled with wonder—
before its oars began to stir,
and with tentative strokes
that grew pronounced
it steadied the wobbly freight of itself
and crested the waves of silvery dew.

# Smokey Gray

*for Scamp, June 21, 2021*

From the throne of a cushion,
a billowing afghan,
you'd sit grooming yourself
as if secure in the knowledge
when I'd come in from shoveling—
tugging on the wet fingers
of my gloves, or stamping snow
onto a runway of old towels—
of who lived the more enviable life.

And those mornings before work
when I'd be packing a lunch—
spreading mustard, making carrot sticks—
you'd have followed me into the kitchen
like a dissatisfied patron grousing to management,
your kibble bowl in need of topping off,
and with each stroke of the peeler
the trill of your complaints—
high and unabashed—
would scrape at my nerves.

But there was another side: your companionship
through a well-pitched ballgame,
a mug of beer in my hand.
Or the way you'd hang like a groupie
when I took up guitar,
blinking through my clunky chord
changes on "Three Little Birds"
as if you could envision them
on the platter of the doorstep—
plump delicacies
with you primed to pounce.

And your turning on its head
that silly notion about feline aloofness
the day our son returned
from the rehab in Florida,
more than a year away
and you sidling up as if he'd never left,
brushing his jeans,
proffering the soft fur under your chin,
then settling beside him
like the friend he could always count on
to abide by the code of dudeship—
never judge or accuse.

# Scrubbing the Chili Pot

After the party, I scour the pot
with a fresh Brillo pad,
my hand gliding up and down,
making swirls and turns
like a skater at a rink.
The grittiest parts next:
congealed beans, a burnt spot
in the center, the handles flecked
as if with a rash. There's reward
nonetheless: my wife, who'd won praise
for her cooking, asleep upstairs—
having earned her rest—
while like an editor with his pencil,
a bassist in a band,
I thrive in the background—
stolid and dependable,
even essential in my role.
When the water goes grimy,
I pour it out and begin again,
a jazz ballad on the radio
while under a flickering bulb—
to no audience or acclaim—
I riff in wee hours, a soloist at the sink.

# Inventing the Mind's Playground

*from a line in a poem by David Livewell*

After washing the dishes
I ball up the foil
that had covered the casserole,
carrying it through the house,
tossing it back and forth
as I stand at the window
or sit watching TV—
through an evening's programs
the hands drifting
across the field of my lap
toward easy liners, under soft pop flies.
Then the fingers moving
with the delicate precision
of someone tuning in a station
or unfastening a lock,
dialing up combinations of pitches:
sinker-slider-circle change.
So many years and the mind,
ever resourceful, returns once more
to those makeshift diamonds
on Windsor and South Redfield
to convert what it can:
bat from broomstick,
crushed tin into plate.
For bases the fire hydrants
and telephone poles,
our obliging kid brothers
we'd anoint going home.

# Little Card

*for my wife on our 40$^{th}$ wedding anniversary*

At the foothills of your pillow,
along the sprawling landscape

of our downy quilt,
I prop the plain brown card

that came in the box
with my new tweed cap.

It vanishes from my sight,
then turns up again—

wedged among the mated socks
in my dresser drawer.

And back and forth it goes:
your handbag, my wallet,

this silly exchange, odd
little volley we keep alive

through household chores,
our days' routines

like a punchline, a ritual
that though worn with use

surprises us still
with its offhand touch.

# Root Vegetable Soup

*for my wife*

When I put on my navy wool coat
for the first time that winter,
I dredge from a seabed of lint
in the right-hand pocket

a peppermint, a lip balm,
a creased grocery list
on which the poet
in me had crafted

with a soft lead pencil
the words *parsnips* and *rutabaga,*
imagery that has me conjuring
here in the hallway—

with new errands to run—
the frosted glass door
and four swaying pines;
snow on the feeder like an igloo,

a watch cap, a domed city church.
And inside the table set
with the everyday spoons
and two Blue Willow bowls

so I can savor once more
the tang of root vegetables
that had simmered on the stove
and misted our windows—

dusk coming on before we knew.

# IV.
Neighborhood, Town, and County

# Walking Lake Caroline

With the coffee shops closed,
and the great pandemic
having set up its yellow barriers—
banning community
even at the community park—
I walk to the lake
just blocks from my house,
learning in these early hours
and after years of driving by
what the men in the reeds
have come to fish for:
perch and bluegill, smallmouth bass.

To listen while wending goose poop
along an asphalt trail
to the falls of the dam
and to a symphony of crickets
as they saw on their instruments;
discern at a foot bridge
what the local poets have inscribed
if not for the ages,
then at least through sophomore year:
*Rat loves BB! Nat is bad!*

To recognize at an overlooked place
the delight of nature in cobbling words:
loosestrife, milkweed, stubbly cat-o-nine-tails
someone described on Facebook
as a swath of corndogs bobbing on sticks.

And which the Lenape discovered
to be perfectly edible, their roastable tips
perhaps the very first junk food
as they settled to their night's viewing—
a people without a cable bill,
sharing the same screen,
gazing at the moon and stars
in those earliest days of public TV.

# With Plaid Thermos While Waiting for a Train

Among our fellow commuters
who stood on the platform
with disposable cups,
such an odd pair we made—
me in my staid combination
of navy and gray;
and you decked out in plaid
like some dorky accomplice
I pressed to my sleeve
as if to keep from view.

But alone in the office
we'd be chums once again,
your cap removed
and the rich aroma
of coffee and cream
reminding me all over
what friends put aside;
that dork or not
you never held grudges
but only hot coffee
I'd sip with avidity—
taking it light.

# Cold Symptoms While Walking at Lunch

Feeling bad felt good in its way—
first a cluster of chills
as a gauge switches on
in the mind's circuitry,
the body emitting
an almost pleasurable shudder;
then an onset of aches
through the sluggish joints
that have me shift
my stride to a stroll.

Such entitlement here.
A time for troubleshooting—
to grade each slope a hill,
each small discomfort
a stone in the tread.
Thinking of the office
with its bottlenecked jobs,
each slip marked *Rush!*
I putter along
like a coddled engine
with the pressure lifted—
riding the brakes and hugging
the shoulder, giving off
an agreeable hum.

# Power Wash

*Holy Saturday afternoon, St. Joseph the Worker Church*

Even saints need tending:
today, along the church lawn,
red and purple geraniums
in a bowed procession
while a worker in coveralls
ministers to St. Joseph—
hoses him down with brass
nozzle and spray.
From a metal stepladder he aims
a hard burst to one side
of his head, rinsing grime
from his hair and beard,
cleaning debris from his ear,
reminding me of those Saturday baths
when we'd be sent with a washcloth
and bar of Ivory
to soak in the tub so we'd be ready
for mass on Easter morning,
dressed in our good clothes,
transformed like St. Joseph
in his spotless robe, the blade
of his ax glittering in the sun,
the jug and crust of bread he proffers,
a mist in the air
that is barely discernible—
hovers a moment
before it spreads like news.

# Stopping Between Errands to Watch Little League Baseball

Forget the hardware store,
the broken clapper
on the running toilet.
And the wilting asparagus,
the half-gallon of mint chocolate
sweating it out
in the sauna of the trunk.
Unlike my fellow spectators in the stands,
I have nothing invested here:
no regard for the score
or, as I'd had years before,
no son to cheer as he stands at bat
or maintains his poise on the pitcher's mound.
But like some roving ambassador,
a retired neighbor filling his days,
I have taken these moments
to play anonymous fan
for both the reds and the yellows
as they compete on the field.
To feel the sun on my arms,
on the back of my neck,
to be a man interrupted—
kindly, avuncular,
without a list or an agenda,
who if only just briefly
on a Saturday afternoon
can put out of mind

the unpacking of groceries
and querulous fixtures.
Can resist even the call
of the pent-up mower—
shrill and exacting,
that disciplines grass.

# Dog Decoys

Sold in packs, they are dispatched
throughout the county—a faint
stir in the air enough to deter
a picnicking groundhog
or rabble of geese.
Durable, they abide all weather,
their silhouettes indelible
on museum lawns, McMansion acres,
or here on the baseball field
where this mottled shepherd
shallow in the gap
between second and first
catches me off base
as I stroll past the gates,
thinking of those easy rollers
that came off the bat.
Across the parched infield
they bounded toward us
before taking a strange hop;
and like our languid summers,
skipped out of reach.

# Playing Catch

And the most touching part
is it's my son's idea—
a grownup now—
to drag out of the closet
the two gloves
and unblemished baseball
with Randy Wolf's autograph.
To go across to the field
and to circle once more
under dizzying pop flies
and stoop for grounders,
to smile as if at an old joke
when one of us tries
to revive a knuckler
or serve up a curve.

After sharing the news
a silence between us
I'd attempted to fill
with the straight pitch
of shopworn assurances:
*caught it early,*
*top doctors, high cures,*
but here in the field
it's easy enough
to settle into the familiar
rhythm of whipping a baseball
back and forth—
father and son a pair of workers,
or like passengers on a ride,

the thud in each glove
as certain as a period
in a declarative sentence
that for now, at least,
is clear, understood.

# At a Turnpike Rest Stop with My Grown Son

*for Andrew, Fellow Traveler*

Only moments ago, on our way to the wedding,
we were snug in the enclave of our well-packed car,
the miles ticking by as we shared the old jokes
with mother and sister, hemmed in
by snacks and suitcases, the sprawled acoustic
in the hard bed of its case, blocking the rear window.
Now, at adjacent urinals, we stare
ahead as if respecting the decorum
of a grittier world where men in silence
come to do their business—ordinary
travelers with a common need.
And here in this place of porcelain and mirrors—
of rank odors cut by disinfectant—
it is easy enough when I close my eyes
to imagine my son a bearded stranger:
in sandals, a red Phillies cap,
but giving off so affable a vibe
I am drawn to wonder what sort
of life he leads, where he might be going,
whether in a different time or place
we might be friends—
my reverie broken as he zips and flushes
and I am reminded of our separateness,
when like a parting son, he moves away.

# At the Super 8

*The loneliness thing is overdone.*
—Edward Hopper, in rebuttal to his critics


The first hot sips from the communal urn,
and with it the thought
that these moments by the windows,
slumped over coffee in a ceramic mug,
might very well be the best in my day.
Early hours with sharpened pencils,
atop a stack of books
poems in a yellow anthology
like assorted pastries displayed in a case.

What difference the wobbly brown table
and mild distractions:
chirpy newscaster, my neighbors
back from the waffle machine—
at any residence the loud family
that makes itself known.
For now, I am in that happy state
somewhere north of departure
and south of arrival,
putting out of mind the uncut grass
and what the cat might be up to, left in charge—
testing the upholstery of the new living room chair.

In a while my wife will join me,
and we'll lift the lids
on the scrambled eggs and vat of oatmeal.
We'll sit together, yet apart,
the two of us turning pages,
only half aware of rain on the windows—
the gentle taps as if to prod us along.

Under the pink neon of the motel sign,
in a patch of light worthy of Hopper,
a man emerges with a single bag—
lonely, or merely alone,
who'd presume to say?

# Itinerant's Song

*for Mary*

My sister without wheels spends
part of her earnings
on trains and buses, puts up
at frilly bed-and-breakfasts,
as if paying to play.
Along the dim corridors, on steep
depot stairs she is overtaken
by the brisk and impatient
as she bears the weight
of an overnight bag
and swaying instruments—
guitar and dulcimer, the bodhran drum
tucked under one arm.
But up on the stage the little amenities
each host sets out by the mic on the stand:
sparkling water; zinnias in a vase;
behind a bow window
a garden at dusk.
And on hard metal chairs
the devotees of the folk scene
who in the fading light
will see the moon emerge
like a tarnished silver dollar,
and through the evening's performance
the glittering stars.

# Errands with My Father

Days, weeks after my father died
he was still giving his dismissive wave
for delayed lights and the squawking
box at the gasoline pump;
for the uninhibited and self-assured:
radio talk show callers;
a power walker making a drama
out of exercise—
flapping her arms on a public street.

In the produce aisle at Acme,
I took his input while gathering ingredients
to make a salad—keeping things basic
with the spring medley and cherry tomatoes,
sliced cucumber in vinegar and oil
I'd serve to my wife
just as he had served to my mother,
setting before her with a sprig of tenderness
her allotment of fiber in a plain white bowl.

Later, in the waning hours of the afternoon,
he led me into the living room
where in a chair by the window
I sat enjoying the breeze
along with some beer and pretzels,
a book I'd glance up from
to hear him tell me
(with a wave at eternity)
that things were fine where he was:

the talk show callers muted,
and even the power walkers
no longer offensive
as they glided by with perfect restraint.

# Mottled Scarf Clinging to Bushes

*for Sarah, Capuchin Franciscan Corps Volunteer*

Thinking of germs, I take a few steps
to nudge us along, but my daughter
home for the Christmas holidays
has stopped on our walk
to untangle it from the bushes—
stiff and half-frozen,
with sequins of leaves.
To bring it back to wash and dry,
then place it with care
by the pairs of Timberlands
she bought from the vendor
at his curbside stall;
the little squadron as if awaiting orders
in a line by our front door—
willing, if necessary, to walk
the 600 miles to the shelter in Detroit,
drivers on the morning commute
taking in along the shoulder
of the PA Turnpike that stalwart formation
of yellow work boots, the scarf unfurled
like a banner in their wake.

# White Delivery Truck Caught in Branches

On our street one day
this slapstick scene:
the driver, we can only imagine,
fooling with his cell phone
or scanning for an address
as the big truck drifted
into a web of low branches.

Then the comedy turning
when driver and passenger
like some bumbling duo
in company sweatshirts
and backwards caps
climbed down to enact
the next part of their skit—yanking
at branches, using a hand saw
to hack off a limb
before driving away.

All afternoon we saw it there:
a tree in fall
looking less formidable—
even a little stunned—
its severed extremity
in a flow of red leaves.

# Little Free Libraries

Just turn the wooden latch
and inside a cubby you will find
beside *The God Delusion*
the *Selected Writings of St. Thomas Aquinas,*
a tattered *Crime and Punishment*
bumping up against *Plumbing for Dummies,*
romance novels, a stack of children's books
lying on their sides as if for afternoon nap.
When did I first notice them among us,
sprouting up as they have
at ballfields, among sycamores
on humid Philadelphia streets?
Think of their squarish heads
crammed with knowledge or emptied out.
Think of them gazing at the traffic
through the cataracts
of filmy plastic windows.
Or the selflessness involved,
green paint flecking off
as they stand in all weather
on the post of one leg
for the giving and taking—
for the offering of books.

# The Indian Neighbors

Retired now, they convene in a half-circle—
fanned out on the lawn in aluminum chairs.
Or, in this land of chains where everyone drives—
to the bank, the grocer's, the Dollar Tree—
they break from convention to go for a walk.
Here they are passing our windows
in knit pullovers and plaid summer shirts.
Like philosophers or professors,
they stroll the campus of our block,
pausing to study the phenomenon
of work being done—
new siding, a new roof—
their voices like a murmuring of leaves
as they continue their walk,
their seamed hands, once employed,
now curled or clasped—
in loose half-circles behind their backs.

# Bird Blind

*Churchville Nature Center*

Though it is dark inside
and as close as a confessional,
I have come if not to tell
my sins then to surrender
the news and cares of a day.
To slip, unnoticed,
into this low pew, careful
not to cough, or shift,
as I peer through slats
at the ceremony of birds
taking turns at the feeders.
Here in this peaceable world
as serene and unspoiled
as an illustrated Eden
in a children's bible
I can almost convince
the grudging cynic weary
of stories on NPR
of the lessons in civility
that birds can teach:
chickadee, nuthatch,
and even the jay
in its regal blues
that when seen at a slant—
through half-closed eyes—
stands in the back
with the decorum of an usher,
helping each latecomer
find a seat.

# On Political Divide

Give me back the familiar courtesies
of choosing sides, mid-day
on a sandlot field with a steady pitcher
like a father at a grill,
accommodating each batter
who steps to the plate—
serving up wobbly meatballs.

And the simple remedies
of maintenance and repair:
oil for the mitt, black electrical tape
across the globe of the ball—
mending the broken stitches.

No umpires with clickers.
No coaches clapping along the baselines,
or parents in the stands.
Just the sincerity of our voices
echoing across the field
as we argued fair or foul,
safe or out,
then let the games resume.

# About the Author

Joseph Chelius is the author of four previous collections of poems: *Taking Pitches* and *Row House Yards* (Pudding House Chapbook Series, 2006 and 2011), and *The Art of Acquiescence* and *Crossing State Lines* (WordTech Communications, 2014 and 2020). He is a former Bucks County, Pennsylvania Poet Laureate and was the first-place winner of the inaugural Short Fiction Contest at Bucks County Community College.

His work appears in *Cider Press Review, Commonweal, Poet Lore, Poetry East, Rattle, THINK,* and other journals. A semi-retired editor and editorial director in the healthcare communications industry, Joe and his wife have two grown children and have lived in Bucks County for 32 years.

www.ingramcontent.com/pod-product-compliance
Lightning Source LLC
Chambersburg PA
CBHW022015160426
43197CB00007B/444